WE ARE HOURLY LABORS. NOT PAUPERS.

LAWRENCE D. TAPLAH

authorHOUSE®

AuthorHouse™
1663 Liberty Drive
Bloomington, IN 47403
www.authorhouse.com
Phone: 1 (800) 839-8640

Published by AuthorHouse 12/06/2016

ISBN: 978-1-5246-5351-4 (sc)
ISBN: 978-1-5246-5350-7 (e)

Library of Congress Control Number: 2016920212

Print information available on the last page.

Any people depicted in stock imagery provided by Thinkstock are models, and such images are being used for illustrative purposes only. Certain stock imagery © Thinkstock.

This book is printed on acid-free paper.

Because of the dynamic nature of the Internet, any web addresses or links contained in this book may have changed since publication and may no longer be valid. The views expressed in this work are solely those of the author and do not necessarily reflect the views of the publisher, and the publisher hereby disclaims any responsibility for them.

DEDICATION

M𝖸 𝗌𝗈𝗇𝗌 (K𝗐𝖺𝗇𝗍𝖾𝗁 𝖺𝗇𝖽 S𝗇𝗈𝗌𝗂𝗈) as bestowal of our kinship, Liberian American or African American.

CONTENTS

INTRODUCTION

INTROSPECTIVELY, THIS IS AN ASSORTATIVE reviews of employment at will and vested interest at Lincoln Industries, a private owned company across Rosa Parks Way in Lincoln, Nebraska, U.S.A. from 1999 to 2015. The specificity of these years will focus on the assiduous attention of hourly labors working in the straight line doom as snow flakes on the plain without an outlet. As one with higher level of education, I am not ashamed of working as an hourly labor. My only shame lies in the fact if I have to beg for a job. This conception maybe valid in the eyes of others. Personally, I have a problem with this as I reexamine my work and relationship with this company. To my readers, I will use the word we referring to all hourly labors and probably every one else in the domain of authority or not in position.

I believe employment for anyone regardless of their ethnicity should be a culpable cultivation, if the opportunity is a moratorium to deject all people from various affinity groups, or to measure the capabilities before and after the test of affiliation. These two assumptions maybe arguments to rebuff a proposition use by some people in some cases if not all to promote the regularly repeated litany of certain hourly labor. This condemnation is a trope I in particular and maybe others may want to deny. The culprits found within the domain of authority of this company want people of certain affinity group to remain indentured servants. Indentured servitude is bound by commitment to work for some one in exchange of living or travel expense.

It is incumbent upon every individual to have a desire for work and to perform his or her duty in collaboration with others regardless of personal dislikes. Hourly labors want to work and be taxpayers like any foe in the avenue of virtue as a moral conduct in liberty and implied in the Commerce Clause of the constitution. The sanctity is we are not shadow of liberty, because liberty is the constitutional right that allows every working able individual non denial of job opportunity. We do not need restitution to enjoy the fruit of our labor.

I am not ignorant or arrogant to the challenges at Lincoln Industries. Like any given company or business there are set criteria in hiring individuals for particular jobs. Therefore let it be know that Lincoln Industries has an open door policy for hiring. Nevertheless, there are individuals with non-sequitur behavior of ensuring some particularity of the workforce comprising of the implicit qualifiers in the domain of authority.

This behavior has become a criteria some authoritative figure are concerned with those who are perplexed by the consequence of their divisiveness.

Working at Lincoln Industries is apparently a choice we made. This choice protects our vested interest in the indulgence of employment at will. Our choice to work is overwhelmingly protected by the constitution of the United States, even though that constitution makes no specific reference.

THAT PLACE

THE BELIEFS AND DRIVERS OF Lincoln Industries are the foundation for what ought to occur and how to achieve them. These propositions are mentioned in every meetings and presentation to all customers in business transactions.

"The Beliefs:

> Our people and their unique individual talents are valued.
> Appropriate recognition motivates our people to be successful.
> Leaders create value
> Innovation creates continuous improvement.
> Profitability ensures the survival of our company.
> Positive relationships build loyalty.
> Honesty is essential in all transactions.
> We create value for our customers.
> Wellness and healthy lifestyles are important to our success.

The Drivers:

> Quality in everything we do.
> Productivity improvement is a continuous process.
> On time delivery because our customers depend on us.
> A safe working environment is our commitment to each other.
> Environmental responsibility is our commitment to our communities.
> People development because our people create our success.
> Company growth is the result of providing a superior service.
> Value-added service means doing more for our customers."

The Beliefs and Drivers are ingrained stimulators that are bound by obligation for the company to grasp and to avoid any skepticism of what to do. People are encourage to comprehend these propositions not about who they want to be, but who they are. These propositions should envisage the foundation to set the economic engine into strategic objectives; namely components formulated to develop the people, implement the core excellence, sustain growth, and adjust financial reviews. Keeping this in mind, attainment of employment at will is very essential for the company's workforce now and in the future.

The Commerce Clause-Article 1, Section 8 of the constitution-Congress shall have power to lay and collect taxes. To regulate Commerce with foreign Nations, and among the several States, and with the Indian Tribes. This is a pursuit for implicit differentiation of obligation in accordance with all actions and reactions of employers and employees alike to agree or disagree in protecting their vested interests. The United States Constitution also acknowledges that liberty of all people must be protected for self-determination.

The fortitude of the Commerce Clause justifies people must be able to work at Lincoln Industries or any entity anywhere in the United States of America. This statement does not preclude the fact that required qualification should be ignored because qualified immunity enable individual to grasp the legality and qualification of liberty as a substantive due process within the constitution.

No apology or an excuse is needed in the pursuit of liberty. The substantive due process measures the level of equality that comes from the conceivable will of all actions and reactions. As far as the challenge for freedom has proven liberty is respected for the rule of law.

Liberty allows employees to challenge actions in ways that may cause some upheaval about rights. One of the challenges should be a composite function for employees to seek the requisite for equal access and a set goal for themselves. Additionally liberty and freedom empower employees with an obligation to themselves to form organized union at will.

This book may come across to readers as an inquiry of supposable fact that consists of coincidence in some way. Simply because introspection alone is not only a prevarication of work experiences and thoughts but a profound source of my indebtedness to my African heritage.

The choice I made to be part of this company for sixteen years is to be an interloper with no mask not a pauper.

The purview of our encounter were disparagement for some people but not me.

My passion to work is still the same because I grab the Beliefs and Drivers of the company as a conditional factor for me to stay despite some frustration at times. The Lincoln Industries is not for certain people but all people who desire to work and enjoy the sanctity in human decency and human relation.

When conformity is, people need to work together regardless of their different affinity groups, something seems to change. This likeness can be a standard image for all in the presence of mind without a threat to any affinity group. We need an unchanging conception.

There is certainty in virtue that deserves explanations for my sixteen years of service at Lincoln Industries. I dissipated the habit of hard work paid dividend as I worked along side others from different affinity group to withstand the might and main who are weak and insecure.

They do not deceive me of their abnormality. Therefore to counter their spinelessness, I reached into the zenith of my existence to make virtue part of me. This apperception of virtue is surety for tolerance.

There should be a certain behavior of response to sustain virtue while working along side others who dislike you. People of different culturally constructed principles or different nationalities in the same workplace (Lincoln Industries) have a choice to choose whether virtue is a moral conduct of their existence. People have to work to earn income and benefits for the sustenance of their livelihood.

In the book by Bell Hooks, (Killing Rage, 1995). "On the jobs, when we express ourselves from a decolonized standpoint, we risk being seen as unfriendly or dangerous." This awareness should be depicted as a purpose that to work in any place does not mean you have to mask the illusion of belonging to satisfy the test of affiliation from different affinity group. When you want to whoop it up at that undetermined moment, the conscious choice is freedom to act. That question then comes to mind and if whether you want to work under rage and understand what is expected of you.

There are many reasons why some individuals are afraid to engage in the discourse narrative of work and affinity groups relation.

From a survey conducted among individuals with work experience ranging from 5-47 years about their importance to work for Lincoln Industries, I was surprised at certain responses from many of them.

The first group was individuals who have expertise in various kinds of work. The second group was different individuals selected randomly about their dislike and still working for the company. The results from both groups are not quite fidelity of their insights but a basic indulgence of their inconvincible actions and nothing else. This confirmation is valuable to me and may be to them for many years working for the same company. The inclusiveness and exclusiveness of their biases can be measured.

Allegation may become a rage by individuals at a workplace if the focus is with intent as described in the book (Nickel and Dimed, 2001) by Barbara Ehrenreich. "Sidling up to me one night to engage in a little nativism directed at the Haitian immigrant. I feel like I'm the foreigner here. They're taking over the country." A wave of competition for work is a threat to a person of the dominant affinity group. It does not matter whether the job is to be a cook or a dishwasher. The intent is a settled assumption based on the tenet the foreign-born is depriving him of his qualified immunity which was not enshrined in the Commerce Clause of the constitution. An opportunity has been taken away from him but he is working and liberty is the cause.

Employment is an entitlement, for this reason some working people feel jobs should be available. What they may not understand is whether the forecast of an economy will be encouraging for company to start hiring. A discretion that suggests a convenient insight for people to use in their preference to protect themselves against that value of decadent. A self-flattery

Sometimes companies want to hire but qualified people are else where and difficult to find. This restraint enables the companies to seek specific skills outside their present locale, including recruitment from aboard. Against some companies there have been lawsuit where judges ruled a claim is balanced for conditional factor sum up for unemployed compensation. Probably this is the root of the famous incentive for individual that are laid off. It is also known that the Federal Government has mandate criteria for assistance to people who have slipped into poverty as a condition of human rights.

Most companies have learned that the absence of manpower is against their bottom line and they need qualified immunity for investment.

Even though qualified immunity is not specific in the Constitution in empathy of investment or employment. But there is always request and judges response favorably.

When did the historicity of the company began? In 1952, Dale LeBaron founded the Lincoln Plating after he purchased a small plating business in down town Lincoln. The company then constructed a new facility which included a modern waste water treatment section on a 32 acre of land in Southwest Lincoln between 1973 and 1974.

In 1984, Dale LeBaron selected and appointed his son Marc LeBaron as president, who purchased the business from his father in 1985. Lincoln Plating name changed to Lincoln Industries in 2007as a choice with Marc LeBaron as the Chairman and Chief Executive Office.

Lincoln Industries has used nickel chromium with electricity to put metallic substrates on surface differentiated parts for motorcycles, trucks, vehicles, and manufactured parts. This choice of coating have been a reliable process and a standard applied to obtain business from customers.

In 2012, Lincoln Industries established two outlets-Lincoln Chrome and Lincoln Performance Coating with different in meeting the demand of their customers. Lincoln Chrome is the retailer of high quality chrome exhaust system and accessories for the heavy-duty truck market. Lincoln Performance Coatings are ceramic coatings in high temperature coatings for corrosion and thermal protection.

In 2015, Lincoln Industries acquired DS Manufacturing, Pine Island, Minnesota as a wholly-owned subsidiary. The purpose was to strengthen its capacity in small and large diameter tube bending fabrication solution. During the same year, a marketing research outlet was set up to launch specific product styles from the recent innovation inspired from technology for metal finishing as Khrome Werks.

When companies expansion become large for the sake of size and not added value, the companies should consider the consequence in this context. This succor may be the goal of the company in its ingenuity for the customers and the people who work to make it succeed. The resilience for too big without consistent income and steady growth could be a delusion as well as an obsession.

The elimination of any fear of too big is to sustain the loyalty of reliable customers with a brand and to search for new potential customers.

Where is the edge for income over growth? Actually, edge is quite a bit reliable when income come from service rendered in valuable products that are sustainable from using your core excellence in what is known to grow. No edge for growth is when expanding by general administration for more people with less income and less profit. The edge in research and development of new products can bring new income if customers want. No edge for income is the denial of business venture taken with no return on investment.

Therefore, income and growth are parallel in the economic engine of any company. Income and growth complement each another not deprived them. It is a dilemma to choose which one of the two is necessary in the sustenance of business venture when investment becomes a momentum for income and growth.

Can the subsidiary, DS Manufacturing, the three outlets-Lincoln Chrome, Lincoln Performance Coatings and Khrome Werks become sustainable? Yes. If the focus is tied to the Beliefs and Drivers which relate to high quality standard and service that no other company has. This is why every initiation should always be a conception base on the Beliefs and Drivers as the happenstance to continuingly make the company survive the challenges and competition in every business transactions. This approach will definitely make the subsidiary, DS Manufacturing, Lincoln Chrome, Lincoln Performance Coatings and Khrome Werks.

Excitement is found within the realm of entrepreneur, a historical fact started by the founder Dale LeBaron which has become a continuous hallmark by his son. This goes to say the utilization of talent against comparative skills is the self-assurance of the entrepreneurial economy which has the intuition to take risk.

Entrepreneur cares about intuitive talent and relative skills for good result. This burden on the entrepreneur serves as a motivation and competence in search of any business transaction. Having this reputation with certainty and knowing the task along the way in every moment is a very good business conception to have.

The advocacy of people saying they like to work for this company appears to be an entremets that people eat along side the main course when they are in a restaurant. The excitement here is a full stomach for the same price.

The choice of freedom as maybe applied to the company is where an excitement is found by moving from one job to another with comparable conpensations within the same company. This excitement also serves as a motivating factor for employees to work where there is shortage of workers which is beneficial to both parties.

Chief Justice John Marshall of the Supreme Court of the United States of America gave a historical review of employment in the Contract Clause of the Constitution. In the case regarding the Trustees of Dartmouth College who did not want to retain its incompetent president conflicted the State of New Hampshire Legislatures who wanted the president retain. The argument then arisen as to who has the eminent power in a pre-existing document to remove the president? This is a classical example of enumerated power of Congress and the interpretation by the Supreme Court which is intermingled with States rights. A dichotomy of the constitution.

In the book by Lee Epstein and Thomas G. Walker, (Constitutional Law for a Changing America, 2011). Trustees of Dartmouth College V. Woodward. 17 U.S.(Wheat) 518 (1819). Chief Justice delivered in favor of the Trustees. "But the American people said in the constitution of the United States, Article 1, Section 10, that no States shall pass any bill of attainder, ex post facto law, or law impairing the obligation of contracts. The opinion of the Court, after mature deliberation, is, that this is a contract, the obligation of which cannot be impaired, without violating the constitution of the United States. The judgment of the State Court must be reversed"

The opinion binds employment at will and vested interest as a guaranteed in liberty. The ruling from that case has been used by private businesses and public organizations to employe or to terminate a worker upon their discretion. Workers have used it to leave an employer without any consequent.

That ruling for employment has been a recipe to discipline all participants to use the constitution for empowerment to challenge any misgiving. No matter what happens, it is a choice to seek redress. The resilience for liberty should lived on all time in equality.

The ruling has been a precedence for all private and public entities who hired individual to work are protected in the realm of liberty guaranteed by the constitution.

Should company and people be protected even though the constitution makes no specific reference to it? Yes. Whenever companies don't want you to work with them they often go to great lengths and seek out events which are despiteful and yet legal. For example, they check to make sure whether your attendance is satisfactory when you clock in or clock out on time. How many times did you call out for sickness or whatever reason. The inquiry is to bring attention on you who is doing job they want. They are surprised that you are fulfilling the task which is required of you to do the job. But they want you to quit voluntary so that they can not be held accountable if there is reprimand. You have the confidence of refusing to be lethargy which makes you to be fluent in administrative tactics. Your objective is to remain employed and be available to conduct yourself especially in policies of the company.

The sycophants have to change their aversions and proceed to bring a scandal that you are arrogant and egoist just like them as a way to impose a schedule to work that is very convenient for you. To remain silent and content is not an entrapment but a way to maneuver your conspicuity of envy. You made a promise to yourself to be the best at any offense or defense.

How to contain a culturally constructed principles for all affinity groups in a place of work? Upholding the laws that has been adjudicated for rules and regulations in concomitance of societal bondage. This deliberation is not to remove challenge to status quo but to retain the same semblance of work ethics among the people. The dastardly result should be a motive avoiding indentured servitude behavior by individual in the domain of authority in selecting certain individual for a job. There is nothing else to show but the implementation of the law not a resistance to the law. Employers and employees know that the law provide disagreement so allowing flexibility.

Why is the enactment of laws as public policies? The obvious tactics are every scrutiny of people has been the purpose to belong to a wholesome functioning society. We the people can not be one affinity group but many affinity groups. We the people are descendants of mixed heritage and nothing is wrong to hold unto it within the framework of the law. When the law is used to cull some people out of a job for disrespect, it shows evidence that we have law of definite propositions.

We should be law-abiding citizens with reputation so our offspring can be the retainers.

To hold law consistent and coherent is not like a coin merely to be toss-up, and say head or tail. A bakery owner was fined twice because he wanted his employee to work ten hours per day and sixty hours a week. The State of New York passed a law to regulate people not to work beyond eight hours because of no specific reason. The owner sue the State of New York for violating his rights.

In the book by Lee Epstein and Thomas G. Walker,(Constitutional Law for a Changing America, 2011). Lochner V. New York 198 U. S. 45 (1905). The opinion of the court was delivered by Mr. Justice Peckham. "The general right to make a contract in relation to his business is part of the liberty of the individual protected by the 14th Amendment of the Federal Constitution. There is no reasonable ground for interfering with the liberty of person or the right of free contract by determining the hours of labor, in the occupation of a baker. The judgment of the Court of Appeals of New York, as well as that of the Supreme Court and the County Court of Oneida County, must be reserved and the case remanded to the County Court for further proceedings not inconsistent with this opinion."

The ruling holds liberty as a glove to protect the cold hands of any obstruction which may come to deny employment at will and vested interest. It was signal the probability that lagging economic indicator should not be the sole problem of companies, the City, State and Federal

Governments. The constitution does not allow the rights of people to be violated.

Searching for jobs and the disappearing of jobs are argument about economy of scale. The fact depends on the policy of who is responsible for business development. Every place of work must have a policy of intent well-founded between the company and its people.

The correlation between losing jobs and creating jobs can be a problem when revenues do not meet expenditures. This problem creates idleness and makes some people to behave in a way like their freedom has been taken away and nothing they can do. The fear of losing a job is not a preference for company, government agencies and people. It is losing the means to maintain your self.

A contradiction in freedom is the action taken to justify relationship. Any twist and turn in morality ought to be that conditional factor for the source of self-pity and tolerance. No condemnation only that caveat of when to take the risk and become a guardian to the obligation of freedom.

According to the Philosopher Immanuel Kant in his book,(Lectures On Ethics, 1930). "Neither nature nor the laws determine a free action; and freedom, leaving our actions, as it does, quite undetermined, is a terrible thing. Our actions must be regulated if they are to harmonize, and their regulation is effected by the moral law." The moment an individual makes a decision it must be very clear that the resolution after the decision is binding. A decision could be right and rejected as a challenge to those individuals in the domain of authority at a workplace. For example, the workload is more for one person.

You asked that someone in the domain of authority to find another person to help you. Your request is deny because there is no money in the budget to hire someone else. Now you are fed up with this tactic. The decision to stay in pain or to leave with pride rests on the moral rule of flexibility or inflexible cost.

Should people be hired through the Talent +survey at Lincoln Industries?

Yes, "Talent +survey is a tool we use similar to a backgroud check, reference check, etc. Talent +survey is about 80% accurate about the person and how they would fit into the roles they are applying for. The Talent +survey is not sole determinate if we hire someone but we do rely heavily on it." There is a need for change in Talent +survey. This procedural is a certainty to promote the most benightedness by some people in the domain of authority about hiring people who they are comfortable with. A conscious choice in fortune to have in decidedly which person will be that consensual individual who can do the job. An illusion in the standing image and currently for all the emphasis on norms not capability.

Most people who are hired for physical intense work are hourly labor without any specific job in mind to do and they are put wherever to lift and move parts. For some people in the domain of authority these hourly labors don't have talent but only capability to move and lift parts anywhere. A capability for anywhere. The issue with Talent +survey is not the way of accepting applicants but where to put them to fit in regard to their competency then their qualification.

Why some people in a work place behave like they are more skillful than others?

Because such people are afraid of competition that may come. They want to protect their job by holding onto a fanatical adherence like-wait for me-before you do anything. If a colleague decides to be a trouble-shooter at the time of the absence of the monopolist, there is friction. If the result from the trouble-shooter was very successful, it signifies that knowledge is not a property of skill but of talent. The divergence shows that knowledge is an idea that can be found in the time of need.

Although, some people had argue that knowledge is talent not skill. It is necessary for me to say that knowledge is beneath the surface of talent which can be developed and transformed into skills. Such a expedient move by someone to solve a problem is a priority to have and the determination to cancel-wait for me-moment. To change is to improve for value. That's quest is a requirement.

What is necessary to change at that place? A selective incentive which can drive away the monopoly of knowledge based on privilege. People are not naïve when someone else is applying an argument contrary to bring change by ways of allowing creative thought to emerge from interactions. To wait and let see if the monopolist can finish work on time is a fluke not intelligent. So why should people wait for change to come when change can be made. Therefore, the zeal to have in pursuance of a reliable outcome is the only way to remove skepticism and allow ideas to come from many sources.

Why must you take a job that you can not handled with your skill? Fear to say no. If you are in a working condition where having a job pressing down on you and you can not keep up, you are in trouble. For that job was selected based on appeasement not on your capability to function. This job may be entrench in a way that a particular affinity group must be available for the job. The way of unintended consequent may be the purpose of this job. Some people in the domain of authority want to see disgruntlement by a particular affinity group in that workplace to justify their qualified immunity. These sequesters have a view that employment at will is another way to promote a workforce for window dressing.

Sometimes, it easy to see and wait for that given moment to say what is really going on. Ellis Cose says it better in his book, (The Rage of a Privileged Class, 1993). "Racial discussion tend to be conducted at one of two levels-either in shouts or in whispers. The shouters are generally so twisted by pain or ignorance that spectators tune them out. The whisperers are so afraid of the sting of truth that they avoid saying much of anything at all." No gusty idea.

Since the law of definite propositions can be appropriate in science but not in a workplace, any preference people want to use does not change the situation. The act to be apprehensive of something you know but afraid to do anything about it, is fear. This anticipation of not willing to say anything is the same as saying nothing.

Does preference plays a role in who to hire for a job? Yes. The selection is expectation in sharing what to believe is well. People will repeatedly ignore the consequence of their action ever if the selector is not suitable for the job and relation between the various affinity groups. This does not stop the enthusiasm by intention to create a masquerade of sequential reasoning where people are not continually surprised about who the job was given.

Is preference a yard stick to measure qualification? May be when making gutsy decision can make a different even if you were not preferable. You have to go to work and continue to behave like there is no problem because you are part of that property of affirmative action. You argee with the structural constraint of nihilism in the discourse narratives by Cornel West in his book, (Race Matter, 1993). "For as long as hope remains and meaning is preserved, the possibility of over-coming oppression stays alive. The self-fulfilling prophecy of the nihilistic threat is that without hope there can be no future, that without meaning there can be no struggle." In this darkness, our existence is to reexamine what have affirmative action done for us and what is it still doing for us who are descendants of African heritage. Our destiny is not to improvise but to improve ourselves with resources.

We must not diminish our strength in ourselves of our quest to be dislodged of our kinship as citizen of the United States of America. This promise to show our affection is to grow in the comprehension of identity. We must make the advantage for ourselves more reliable without an excuse. Such an obligation is available for us to be responsible for our own success. We must use the system based on liberty.

Where is the confrontation if we oblige to salute President George Washington of the United States but oblique not to salute President Barack Obama of the United States? Our comfort is in the consanguinity of our affinity group not the kinship as citizen. People are struck in their ways as a conviction of belief to be a guilty bystander.

What is the problem of comfort with confrontation? It is concerned with those who are perplexed by the consequence of their heritage. This notarization is a clue to real and lasting change which are sustained by the relationships we build with one another as individuals..

2

NOW WHAT

LOOKING INSIDE THE BASKET IS to find out whether any application is there for a suitable choice in specific kind of job. Most of these applicants are hourly labors with an entry level positions as electroplater, forkfilt operator, inspector and many more. The effort of these hourly labors across the production lines are to meet the supply and demand of customers for their various parts. The excessive use of coercive tactics are having harsh impact on how hourly labor adapt in a way they endured tarry in order to meet whatever was described for them.

The whole drift of escalating effort is to impose restriction on hourly labor not to earn as much money as salary labor. Attempt by some people in the domain of authority is a reality with passion that every once in a while they make every effort to combat no change as a vantage point for them to define or refine the responsibility of hourly labor. A specificity to design a policy of need and not want.

Is there a look inside the basket for policy? Yes to advocate the importance of hourly labors as lesser participants on the chart of the cost of living index. Hourly labors are aware that the cost of living is manageable by getting up every day for a job to go to. This surety is more appropriate at a company, private and public organizations for income and benefits. If they are unable to find work at such places, they choose another alternative as a-live in-at the same home with their employer under the conditional prudence of-rent free, food, and possible restrained transport. This option is indentured servitude that painful way out for cost of living. A derision from one job to another with the same outlook for the working poor.

A point of illustration in the book by Toni Morrison, (HOME, 2012). Cee is asking her friend Thelma about getting another job because her income is not enough to live on.

Thelma said, there is a job if you can handle it. Cee went for interview and accepted the job as a-live in-to be a helper to the doctor. "Cee loved her work: the beautiful house, the kind doctor, the wages-never skipped or short as they sometimes were at Bobby's." But when Cee got sick it was a different experience because there was no health insurance even though she was working for a doctor. He did not want to take her to the hospital when he fails to treat her and for another doctor to treat her.

Frank receives a letter from Sarah, the house keeper of the same employer of Cee saying your sister is ill, "Come fast, she maybe dead if you tarry." Upon his arrival at the house Cee was unable to move herself so he had to pick her up and put her in a car. He took her to their home town to seek medical assistance from the ladies who are herbalists.

After Cee got well the ladies told her these words, "Don't let Lenore or some trifling boyfriend and certainly no devil doctor decide who you are. That's slavery. Somewhere inside you is that free person I'm talking about. Locate her and let her do some good in the world."

What connection is there between work and the peculiar condition of hourly labors as they think through their experiences. The masquerade of virtue can completely disappeared before they realized their own fate in this callousness of supply and demand. From these experiences hourly labors are aware that somebody else has to look inside the basket and thrust upon them what they need as much against their livelihood and regardless of their aptitudes.

Why is this intolerably heavy burden of doing for need is not for want? Hourly labors must work for a company even if they do not like some people of the same company who may think they have the authority to decide the schedule of work. There must be no doubt about this. For experience has no underlying significance but only a drift of circumstances by self-consciousness. There is no point of reference outside which can determine the relative value of competing policy to alleviate constraints. This is why freedom in liberty is paramount to hourly labor that it is difficult to remain warmly convinced by the impromptu statements of policy which may be obeyed but nobody seriously regard them as having authority. As the matter of daily experience all policies have to be within the occurrence of the Commerce Clause.

What is endangered when freedom is mixed with passion?

When people pride and hope are viewed as happiness. An account of how pride and the denial of hope have become the central motive in human destiny. Pride enables people to realize some of their hopes. But it offers no guarantees that they can be fulfilled. The arrangement of conduct by consent can be obedience to achieve pride in happiness but not a reward in hope only a conscious effort to find a way to virtue. For there is no limit.

Perhaps, no particular view endures protection where illusion is when hourly labors cannot reconcile what they know with what they must set up for. Some insight can lead to that conclusion-we have to work under rage to understand what is expected of us.

Hourly labors have to rise when desire comes to them which does not accept the necessity of putting restraint on opportunity. For desire depends on how much there is to take into account the simple thing which is inherently absurd to some people who have an ingrained habits.

What do customers want from Lincoln Industries? They want their ferrous metal such as steel, stainless steel, iron and nonferrous metal such as aluminum or brass to have different coating on them. This is the kinds of work Lincoln Industries can do by applying electricity with nickel chromium and others on those metal parts into finishing products. The handlers of these demand are the physical intensive Scout around the production lines and the covert Scout in cubicles. These people are like eager beaver who are obligated to fulfill the needs of customers.

Can there be another kind of work beside nickel chromium? Yes, making metal devices by fabrication for manufacturing. Although the production is small in quantity but it is a focus on which the company cannot refute. The predilection is whether customers will appreciate these new sensuous products and be convince. Once there is no disruption in nickel chromium parts, the customers are not disincline to listen but they want to be in charge to make the choice of what kind of products they want.

Does Lincoln Industries have to wait to conduct research? No because the taste of customers changes. The company has to step up with innovation to grab that taste which is important for who they are and what is available. Having an edge in electroplating is not the only process to make this company great. A productive workforce with strategy objectives can put the change into where the company wants to go.

This assertion is not a hollow but a fork in the road to be removed when procedures are institutionalized.

The underlying demand for people with abilities is to transfer their capacity for skills which maybe useful without hindrance for the kinds of work they want.

When ability is not put in use to develop skill, it causes productivity to slow down. Skills are preparatory function taken in to do a job as a choice of an individual or a company. Without bias skill can be taught for a job but not ability. Skills are those particular methods in use at the maximum of performance.

What is the different between ability and talent? Ability is a habit like a tendency to be willing to work when you make yourself available to accept a job conditional. The ingrained action of people is ability not talent. People want to use their ability to survive than to fit their talent into the job. Waiting for the presumption of talent only to be displayed doesn't give you a job to do. Ability is a commitment with confidence to have which will guarantee you a job. Talent is that desire beneath the surface of know-how waiting to be exposed or develop into skills.

Can talent be found in qualification or competence? Yes in competence, talent is a process that takes time to develop as the right stuff into skill for the job. No in qualification, because talent is not acquired through academic or on the job training. Talent is having knowledge with hope to be develop into skills which makes a person to perform and transform in strenuous ways. Here are examples of talent into many years of practice as skills-Medical Doctors, Nurses, Lawyers, Engineers, Athletes, Educators, Police Officers, Soldiers and many others. For people at Lincoln Industries talent is what you bring with you for readiness to work. If you have to work around the production lines you will be train to become an electroplater. A fancy name for hourly labor.

What is electroplating? "It is an electrochemical process where metal is deposited onto the surface of another object. This is typically done with low volume DC current. In a typical plating line, the parts to be plated go through a vigorous cleaning process to remove all organic and inorganic material that may be on the surface. Controlling the chemistry of the plating bath is critical to maintain the correct balance and assure the process works well." The easy interpretation is putting raw metal after they are polished on a rack and them into small or large tanks with chemical for a certain period of time while electricity is apply.

The result of the process is to make the metal parts into a finished product for use in many areas.

What electroplating a metal means? "Adding a thin layer of one or more metals to a base surface that changes the appearance and the properties of the original surface." The metal spoons, knives, and forks are plated and are used to eat and door knobs. This distinct coating is to cover differentiated metal products for good permanence and longevity.

Why is electroplating necessary? "To increase the life expectancy of the products, improve paint adhesion, increase electrical conductivity, and alter or enhance the cosmetic appearance." Example, electroplating nickel chrome makes the surface bright and shiny. Zinc plating on nuts and bolts. Automotive and agricultural parts to prevent rusting. Cadmium is used in aviation and aerospace application to improve corrosion protection. You can take this example as a Nebraskan. During the winter season, people put on winter gear as protection against the cold and to keep warm all the time until the winter season. You can not ignore this preparation for illness. Therefore, it is necessary to keep yourself warm. That's durable and doable.

What is fabrication? "Manufacturing raw tube in different processes such as tube bending, end forming, slotting and welding operation to make a finished assemblies for Class 8 trucks and many more." In other words, cutting and twisting raw metal into products with minimal defects and polished for electroplating.

What is the different between assembly and packaging? Assembly is taking subcomponents and putting them together. While packaging is just boxing up a product for customers. The importance of assembly and packaging is having parts in a one stop shop for all products that customers don't have to search for elsewhere. The difference is it saves time for customers to do some other things.

How is flexibility handle with customer's demand? Priority is given to parts that go through the production lines not on schedule. A typical demand for extra effort is done by chance to rush and to please the customer. We let to make sure the customer is satisfied when the chance is available to make a request based on demand.

Is there a benefit to polish some metal parts before electroplating? Yes. It depends on the customers requirement and the manufacturer of those parts. Some parts are used for both cosmetic and corrosion protection. Polishing is a critical means in differentiated metal finishing. It is putting sandpaper on a big machine to remove roughness and stains from raw metal parts so they can be smooth for electroplating. This is not as waxing vehicle tire rim or putting a coat on shoes with a small brush or a cloth for clean and shine.

What is performance coatings? The applying of coatings in spray booths with the use of clean dry compressed air to atomize properly the coatings. Example, Cermets provide high temperature corrosion and thermal fatique protection of cover metal for usage in racing cars.

Why Lincoln Chrome is an opportunity for customers? A choice for people looking for specific exhaust which is different from the original exhaust coming from the factory for their trucks. This is the option for particular customers for their new or used truck. An advantage customers look for which makes a difference in the way their trucks look special.

How do Lincoln Industries encourage customers ? By asking questions about the function of the parts: base material, hardness of the metal, critical areas and dimensions; the size of the parts that helps determine if the parts needs to be racked or barrel plated. Providing customers with the various needs to understand before any work is done. This ease any tension that may come later. The involvement of customers is not an insistence but a purpose to be trust-worthy. This awareness of coming together leads to honesty in all business transactions.

Is there another way to encourage customers? Yes. Working closely with them in the design phase of their parts and build a relationship that leads them to seek you out to solve their problems. Customers deserves cooperation and trust not liability. This echo of creating a choice makes Lincoln Industries to provide opportunity and privilege for customers to express their inordinate command over work and commitment to the services they want and need. A value for success comes from exchange of ideas about the product.

Why the inclusion of many people from different kinds of work? For their thoughts and expertise in subjective criteria that are needed to capture the basic skills at this company.

I hereby express the importance of the skills which have made this company a competitor in metal finishing. A very crucial connection between the people and their work is a reference obviously related to the cause of this company to remain in business.

It is amazing to know these workaholic are virtuous in doing what they consider to be a clear mandate to meet any obstacles that may come their way.

Holding such a confidence in their skills to maintain their abilities is ingenuity. These people are conscious of employment at will as an indicator that allows them to do their work with passion.

The demand of why we have to work under rage is to understand what is expected of us based on the deontological argument about the obligation of morality. To work is to be steady in getting up and doing the responsibilities required of you.

Can I say more about these people and their work? Yes, no matter our affinity groups of differences we are the same people and I am part of them. Therefore, we are what we make of ourselves to have that behavior to compete and seek to succeed. Underlying this confidence is the work we do and our commitment to the company. We like our various jobs.

What are the benefits people received when they are hired at Lincoln Industries? Beside wages, Medical, Dental, Vision, Life insurance, Uniforms, Steel toes shoes, paid vacation days, Profit Sharing, 401K retirement plan, Gym with a Healthy Unit for wellness and also an Educational Assistance Program to attend any college in Nebraska. There is a monthly Champion lunch for all three shifts and once a year dinner in celebration of our success, achievement and service that we called Night of Champions.

SETTLED ASSUMPTION

A DISPOSITION BY PEOPLE IN a certain way with experience, conception, and ideas to be in control. This disposition is not a resentment but a worthy cause sentiment that flows to humble the pride of people in decision making.

It is a summation of their vested interest to change or not to change values of people. Such imposition is in defiance of all sorts of illusion and distortion that twists understanding into the fixation of sentiment. This requirement has absolved all capabilities into a tenet which can become virtue. No consequent for identity.

In a book by Derrick A. Bell, (Faces at the Bottom of the Well, 1992)."Crucial to this situation is the unstated understanding by the mass of whites that they will accept large disparities in economic opportunity in respect to other whites as long as they have a priority over blacks and other people of color for access to the few opportunities available." Such action is a settled assumption about knowing what to do and how to protect yourself within the system. A cry to hold that tenet in the realm of liberty.

The aim of settled assumption by people is to put that understanding into a practice at a place of work. This tendency gives you confidence in doing a job with privilege at that moment without opposition. People are not wrong about their resiliency to work under rage and surround in any given situation of nostalgia. We who are bestowal of African Americanism know as a fact.

It is refreshing to see settled assumption of people at Lincoln Industries during meetings. Most of them use their exemplary inputs to ascertain evidence of confusions and doubts about what is actually going on within this company at two meetings. Round Table is one with scheduled once a month where every body is invited regardless of your position and One Company One Voice twice a year. Every proposition avails for discussion is in a format of questions and answers about the company's business, the people, the core excellence, the growth and the financial review.

What a qualified person must do to be offer a position? "Look at the job description to evaluate your capability to perform the job. Higher education is a plus but not having a degree doesn't exclude someone from consideration." These are proposals so naïve that it is not worth examining its impossible criterion. The conceivable choice is based on who is in the domain of authority and wants to declare a position. This request is essential for some people to hold unto the strength of the organizational structure of the company. The method is an attempt not to make error in the consequential appearance of creating equity at the company. This consideration of preference is not wrong as a denial in the shadow of liberty.

What is the purpose of that test of affiliation? To provide access as a mean to the law for everyone. Some people don't give a darn how long you have been working with them. All jobs have a level at which experience and education achievement should be useful but it doesn't matter.

How do we continue to integrate everyone to belong? "The easy answer is good leadership and adhering to Lincoln Industries-Beliefs and Drivers. We want to make sure we don't design a bureaucracy." Here again, the surety is the open door policy to invite any one to come and apply for a job just like a- comfit sour candy-in a grocery store. But we also know a workplace is not a clubhouse that forbids intergation of descendants of different affinity groups. This negation does not enfold the Beliefs and Drivers. But it is the quiet fidelity of some people largely being devoir.

Where do we start to unfold? By communicating with people, formally and informally. Hereby creating an environment where they feel recognized and valued. The need to focus on promise and a gift of relevancy verifying we are all part of this together.

Can we really improve the lag of communication among us? Yes, if trust is transparent. This echo for trust would be a burden to share and should be neutral. The involvement of everyone to express himself or herself freely and about evadable aversion levitates potential problems. Trust is a conceivable tactic people use in relationship. It becomes a fixation on people to not behave and makes people behave badly when working under rage and are unable to express their frusration.

How open is Lincoln Industries to employing foreign-born people? "There are many different nationalities hired that are from different cultures and consider them to be a valuable addition to the workforce. We think this is one of our strengths." The inference is well that Lincoln Industries initiates an open door policy to allow foreign-born into its workforce should be commendable. This shows accountability in the Commerce Clause of the constitution is not in a pendulum jowl? Because the point is that each foreign-born has an opportunity to engage in work and earn income with benefits which not a coincidence.

It is imperative that foreign-born have to work under rage to understand what is expected of them. The writer of this book is a foreign-born from Liberia on the West Coast of Africa.

An alumnus of Sacred Heart University, Fairfield, Connecticut and a former Graduate student from the University of Nebraska-Lincoln.

How to keep the culture that we have? "It is important to always treat people with respect, and this goes back to the type of people that we get-smart people with a good work ethic, but who don't put themselves above other people."

Really. A code of altruism from the Beliefs and Drivers for how people ought to behave. We are still waiting to exhale the pain of contention and trust that has been a habitual sequence inflicted on us by some people in the domain of authority who are careless. We the outsiders have to make a diffence even if we are not rewarded. We can refurbish our behavior of who we are instead of what we want to be. The appreciation of working is not a signal for congratulation for our service but acknowledgment of the service rendered.

Why should clownery expatiates daily at work as a joke on affinity groups? To reduce tension and or to promote tension in the cause of bias and civility. The behavior is inexcusable and annoyance. Most violators of such behavior do receive warning immediately but are not dealt with until the frivolous excuses become an embarrassment. An investigation is always conducted to find out whether the behavioral pattern of the clown was the same in the past as the present. The cause to act is delay until the affection is unbearable. The remedy that comes after the fact is, the choice to transfer the clown to another area and wait to see if the behavior will change or not is not gusty.

Can there be reduction in the workforce at any time? "Yes, based on the needs. Some people may be asked to either leave voluntary or be terminated." Everybody is aware that employment at will is a systemic preferment.

The reduction in the workforce spares some people during recession and the slow down of business activities. This request can change the plan of the fiscal year when sales and revenues are dropping and the budget is overhead.

How do we prepare for new businesses? "Look for those that are finishing intensive, high volume, and hard to do. Find companies that are compatible with our culture. By so doing we want to stay entrepreneurial, and build off of what we know best to do." To stay in the entrepreneurial economy requires a vestibule school. But the realm of an entrepreneur is a cause to act upon an idea from wanting to do something about it. This source of idea should be a distinctive fit in order to put into practice the development of product.

When the achievement of the entrepreneur is accepted, change in the product as well as the people who want to work. An entrepreneur will take risk at an undetermined moment to make a change in business from that long research of ideas.

What is the expectation of people at work? "When people have a clear expectation of what to do and how to do it, they are more willing to take ownership." A brave notion to get the right people ensure they are trained correctly, and that they understand the expectations. To accept a job from this company should be a dedication upon an imitation that allows a duty will be perform. The entanglement of people behavior of freedom to do what they want not what they need. Only workaholic not whims meet the demand of this company. It is always fun coming to work and seeing others going home after their hours with pride and dignity.

What is the problem about the retention of people? "There have been no identifiable theme, such as pay or roles, but in several instances those people did not see opportunities for advancement internally within two to three years." Disengagement is a fact. People leave because they have been tired of disgruntlement. When people are concern that nothing have been done to stop nepotism base on an affinity group, it is a clear signal to seek the exit.

Animosity is another factor which baffle people about moment of undesirable behavior and make a person wanting to leave. Employment at will and vested interest are cleaved into liberty so people can leave without consequent.

Why are people reminded to be familiar with the Beliefs and Drivers? To comprehend the Beliefs and Drivers is not a restating of words that people must say as a recitation. These propositions are code to examine whether morality and work relationship are coexistence in the workplace without the lost of business transactions.

Should people in authority be accounted to uphold the Beliefs and Drivers? Yes. "We have had situation where all the guys on a line have only been there a short time, or are new, and people get burned out because there is a lot to learn and lot of pressure. There is no one to help them progress." An example of expecting unskilled people to perform. The ripple effect from trained people to any able body who want to work. These people can be replaced at any time. This notion is an incentive use by some people in the domain of authority to justify what they know as managing cost.

Why the use of unskilled people is important to control cost in production?

Absurdity and alienation are not okay for selective appeasement in a place of work. This is negligence and shameful. There is a notion that hourly people are not ambitious enough to develop the skills that are requested and valuable. Some people in the domain of authority don't care where they put these hourly people to work because they behave it is not hurting the company. What a regret after financial review.

Is there a distinction for people with productive talents and skills? Yes, some individuals are resentful, become anxious to drive others away; a selfish notion that they are the only capable ones to rely upon. This behavior stamps from the fact that others are capable of performing the same job with credulity. The competition challenges create the resentfulness for fear of taking my job.

Competition makes people nervous and therefore is not accepted. Individuals that are pathetic and whims hide behind friendship and lies. They behave like civil servants in government agencies and their actions should be considered as malfeasance. This nuisance must be dealt with as the option exenterate waste and tap talents somewhere else. Competition provides distinction.

Why will people want to work at Lincoln Industries? "It is fundamental to create a place where people want and desire to come to work 4 out 5 days feel fulfilled 4 out of 5 days. We spend 8-10 hours here every day." People want the root of character building, work ethics, and values that are engrained in some people who have been with this company for many years. People want to explore whether they can develop those attributes or learn how to acquire them.

The Beliefs and Drivers are so important to this company because it is the composite structure and the mandate enshrined in the overall activities. This place of work should not be a mandate for only producing goods and services. It should also be a community of settlers who come everyday to share their wants and needs. I am hoping everyone can realized their potential and participate despiteful of drudgery at times.

Why is profit sharing so important to the people and the company? Profit sharing is based on workers productivity and performance versus assets of the business. This has lead to the restructure of profit sharing. The current plan is a better design equally so we need better and transparent communication.

The return of profit sharing in the form of extra payment back to workers is significant. The dividend brings out disagreement between workers around production lines and others in various cubicles. The problem is equitable distribution not on the base of income but a pool.

Do we earn the same amount in wage or salary? No, we do not earn the same amount why should we have the same amount. We can dive in the pool for water or cash the same time but can not come out with the same in our hands. Equity is measure in asset not access.

The echo of inequity is an extenuation of priority about who make the decision for profit sharing. In the book by Robert H. Frank and Philip J. Cook, (The Winner-Take All Society, 1995). "In relative terms, however, those who specialize in highly repetitive production tasks have been losers in the process, while those who oversee the results have been the winners." To justify which group has the privilege to determine priority is very difficult for me to say. I am a hourly labor around the production lines. Making profit is a certainty of doing business. The sharing of profit is based on the policy of each company. Therefore, profit sharing is worthwhile despite the unfair distribution. The concern of people is always the amount received for profit sharing is not enough. Will it ever be enough?

What do we need to do to have more profit sharing? "Everybody has to do what they are expected to do; that results in more productivity, which creates more profitability. Hopefully that will drive individual performance." This demands of people to be more productive in composite function of their work is a prospect for expectation as a guesswork if the outcome is right or wrong. The certainty is where to find accountability and who to blame if profit is not made to be shared.

Can the business be double by sales or growth? "We are always looking at our options. We also need to look at how we use our space. We have to have deliberate intent with any changes made." The only strategy is in vying for the handling of materials in volume for sales, instead of looking for new business to grow and fill the space. The concern should not be only for sales but for growth as well.

How to keep train people? The company needs trained workers across the various areas.

"Therefore, there is a need to develop a curriculum that provides on-going training for those that transferred. Subject matter expert needs to be developed to ensure that training is timely." This approach leaves a wide latitude for individuals in the domain of authority to be selective of the type of workers they want to train.

Repetitive work for some workers is not a conscious choice of boredom but a way to sustain their abilities for livelihood. Every time some else makes a decision for workers may not be a straight line in developing skills. Getting workers skillfully prepared for intended job transfers is the best way.

The push to train workers for different areas within the workplace is a comparative sign that the company appreciates its workforce. Notwithstanding the excuse for push and pull of workers in all directions has been imperative for divisiveness by some individuals because of the range of rant from affinity groups. No matter the excuse retraining workers that are formalize with the job needs to be carried out an indication that the company is mindful of continuous education for enhanced performance and non complacency of workers.

Who hires the lack of train people and put them whenever and wherever to work? Individuals in the domain of authority responsible for assigning workers wherever and whenever without specific instruction or direction should be held liable for having lack of trained workers. This flimsy choice does not fulfill the requirement needed for a job and leads to disaster.

This habit of need is just another way of a conceivable knowledge of ignorance without the core competency to do the work. It is not okay. The thrust to hire any able body to accelerate the movement of parts from the production lines is not only a call to work but a duty to perform.

Is there somewhere else to look? Yes, the innateness of some people to be less responsible for their impulsive belief in hurry of nothing particular but to feel good of themselves. This foundation is emotional in their decision making.

To be thorough for the moment is to treat work like a built-in relationship not a habitual sequence. Instead, too often it is the habit to survive that is the relevant factor not because of someone in the domain of authority.

Should people in the domain of authority be held responsible for their habit of hiring any able body person as a necessity to work? Yes, they like to take the chance to avoid competition. These same people believe that taking a chance may enable them to be lucky to find someone suitable for the job.

Why do people have to work? To establish the basic complement of their talent and skill in exchange for compensation such as income and benefits. To work is also an opportunity to utilize some finite time in activities of the 24 hours per day.

A desire for work is a demand that people must have. Doing the work gives us that freedom of choice from the base of our existence. To work is not a chance of obligation from whatever but a responsibility to have and to hold. When you are aware of your heritage in a workplace where you are not part of the dominant affinity group, you must become an interloper. If you don't you will work dejectedly in that place of sorrow. If you want to be joyful, the test of affiliation with people in the domain of authority is an illusion to have at that place of work. But a necessity.

How many twists and turns should an interloper encounter before making a choice to leave that workplace? There is none to be calculated. You know your commitment is not a blind obedience like an indentured servant. To work only to be sure you feel no inclination to receive an award. This achievement from not depending on the evaluation of you by someone else is the value of your existence. You know the sacrifice of your service to maintain a job and the circumstances which made you a reliable worker. You can throw up your hands and say to yourselves, it was fun.

How to exist from what you have enjoyed doing? In hindsight you remember everything and precisely the pain and degradation you had endeavor with daily smiles. A recognition of your desire to be positive. If you had to wait for that whisperer who is invisible, and yet untouchable in the search of fulfillment, you will be mad. But you know that is not for you. Now you can laugh and say to yourself, I'm not a fool.

Where to find the entrance for your anguish and anger despite your success?

It was not been different even when you were silent and unquestionable about caring so much about liberty. To exist in such a way was your opposition not to be a defender of your affinity group like them.

An oath you kept to yourself. This signifies to you every way in which you have realized your effort never to be intimidated by any one. To accept the whisperer who is invisible is easy. You must move on the entrance is near don't look back for memories.

SOMEWHERE

Awakening after sixteen years working at Lincoln Industries have been an uphill battle of situations to stay centered during difficult times.

Could I be ignorant of restriction that serves the intended purpose of belonging to an affinity group? Yes, restriction functions in people with contradictions of norm that has apparent root. This is the bind to be an interloper at the work- place with self-assurance of knowing what is expected of you, as worker under rage. The job has being under review by some individuals who already have their own job yet desire yours. They blame you for having a job in the same workplace without showing humility the very secret of obedience.

What to do to examine the road ahead? You are holding unto a job which strikes them as strange for someone of an affinity group they dislike. If you don't work well with them, it doesn't work well for you in the long run.

The fault-finding is you are responsible for the non-sequitur behavior that gives you self-confidence to be yourself. Your concern to remain on the side depends on nobody else but you. The road is not that far away keep on looking for the entrance.

Why is the availability to express doubt in a way of not knowing is a certainty only in private? I know most people have the liberty to express themselves but fear illustrates how problematic it is to proceed from that settled assumption.

Some people are not willing to muster their exact thought in public like what I am saying in this book. Everybody is mandated to examine himself or herself and be able to evaluate whatever is going on with work and affinity group relations. A cue to liberty.

Is work and relationship of people from different affinity groups the argument?

Yes. Unanimity is measure in how each affinity group has a choice in liberty to choose whether to work under rage or not to. Since I am able to work in the values of Americans openness and the rule of law, there is no way to hide the promise of liberty for all. Refusing to allow the opportunity to make a difference should not be a dread but an aspirations.

The point is human disposition can not just be a tendency to act in certain manner but a responsibility for that action. This distinction is the choice to make. An explanation is clear in the book by Tommie Shelby, (We Who Are Dark, 2005). "Caring consideration of how a given policy, procedure, or practice will impact the relative life prospects and political power of different racial groups must be a component of any antiracist agenda." The resolution of any policy is to have directions and evidence of liberty in employment at will. A virtuous plea. This quest is the imperativeness of morality. The appreciation of want as a base to work under rage and understand what is expected of you is always a conscious choice. In deciding where to work and when to leave that place of work does not put liberty in handcuff.

What is the accomplishment about writing this book? To say it my way. There is something to be said about having a mind-set of not being a guilty bystander in what I finally accept as the given in my existence; Liberty for an African descent. I like the mental fortitude and the determination to pursue the promise of liberty for me to earn income in exchange of rendered. This is the option of equal access to know what is liberty and how to use liberty. I am saying why I had to work under rage to understand what is expected of me as a hourly labor at Lincoln Industries for the past sixteen years. So far my description of those definite time frame serves the reality of me having fun doing different kinds of jobs and waiting to exhale.

Where is the rage to understand what is expected of me at work? It is found through the rein of credulity through selective choices. Some people hope that I will respond with possibly leading to meanness become victim they want to find. Therefore, the only way for me is to flow and face the hollow of certain people mental disposition of reality. I'm trying to control such a behavior and this is the way I know how to do it. The consequence is often my comprehension of a status of naught a value. Maybe there is something else according to Albert Murray in his book, (The Omni-Americans,1970). 'That much of the blackest frustration grows out of being excluded goes without saying, but much of it also comes from having to witness others making a mess of something you are convinced you can do better." You must wait.

Is there a priority for nothing? Yes if your insistence is a recall of memory as a missing links which would have made a different than you are right to look back for happy times. But you have to accept this axiom that-you cannot throw away the baby with the bathe water. So what was there for you to stay that long working in that place. Facing many people who you felt were courageous in stopping those bully with virtue in relationship for affinity groups. How shameful is the tenet of those others bully? Their dramatic findings are profoundly influence by reputation of certain sorts of contradiction based on what they care about than what we ought to care for. The tenet is conceited in something where there is nothing.

Do you want to leave the job? Yes, if there is a way to sustain yourself by earning income with benefits. This inquiry is an encouragement to plan for the unknown. The only action you have to take is to take it. If you are afraid then stay on the job until a plan is made. Now you must face the fact that interaction with people who want to know your plan will start asking you some questions which may be to find out if you are intact. They want to disturb your comfort zone for a rout.

Where is your intactness? If your response to this question will make you feel and look like an ignoramus, it is because you know there is a diabolical twist for a result. You know these people will continue to bother you. Some people want you to react with angst so you can become a victim of a bully and nonsense. Therefore you must be aware of the challenge to argue in your defence in public not in private when there is no one but you. This stupidity can be handed with a whip but you are waiting for that undetermined event to use your freedom. You wait at fooling yourself or looking elsewhere as only you alone have the power to engage when you want to. It is right to be reserved bystander.

The problem is to remain silent about negligence by some people inability to appreciate their responsible for liberty in equality because they want you to be like them in every way possible. Whenever you provide a tantamount negation against their demand they feel insulted and tantalizes the relationship that was to come in the form of unanimity. Since you are only concern about work and affinity groups relationship not a friendship in the comity of equals, you are seen as a jerk who does have the time for socialization after work. You want to protect your worthiness as well as theirs.

It is not a crime or a wishful thinking to protect any affinity group as a convenience choice of identity. So to be jealous is not a responsibility to stand up for but a surety of cowardice.

Why to be separate and equal has an importance to all affinity groups? Because there is conceited recourse for people to remain within their own group and not another group should be a norm. This egocentric is a stand at workplaces and people are accustomed to it. For some people such fondness is a privilege that has a strangle hold of values. But others see such fondness as a waste of time on nothingness.

In the book by Reg Theriault, (How to Tell When You're Tired,1995). "The myth of the lazy black man persist in some quarters, but among those I know who are on lighting at other jobs, blacks far out number whites." Belonging to an affinity group can bring despair in the inadequate allocation of resources to find a job when you are penniless. The primary cause of scarcity must be the basic pride from an ulterior motive not to share or surrender information to others who are not part of your affinity group.

When weighing your option that does not follow a pattern made for you by someone else request. You are not a pauper. You have been working but they just don't want you around because of who you are not what you are doing. Some people want you to have a pitiful conscience of having a job and not be pompous of doing the job. Example, lifting a pipe from a cart and putting it on a rack that is on a bar to be taken away by a hoist. Taking a broom to sweep an area, a mop to clean a floor or empty the trash can. These examples are simple and necessary to show where completion of the work does not rest on skills but ability to perform. .

Is there privilege for anyone in the Beliefs and Drivers of Lincoln Industries? No, but some people in the domain of authority and even those without position of authority behave they have it to misuse their so-called position.

Most people know that it is wrong but some people still want to resist that member of certain affinity groups have privilege and nothing those who are not member can do about it. The chance to change that concern of privilege is to come in the interplay of consciousness and motivation. They don't want to ignite this change but to remain in darkness.

Is there a conditional factor for diversity in the workforce? Yes to uphold the Beliefs and Drivers in this way-our people and their unique commitment-is all we want. This act of awareness is a realization of privilege at the expense of all the people. No culprit want to redefine the Beliefs and Drivers or abuse his or her freedom of choice in liberty.

Should gratitude be consider when you work for income? No, because gratitude is a temperament to cope with people but not a function that determines your capability to do a job. Gratitude makes you to behave differently and serves as motivation but does not offer you job.

Sometimes, if you are not of the same affinity group, you must appreciate a job as a gift from the company not an obligation to you. A job of appreciation has a conditional factor in the mist of people who don't want you around. Because you are not a member of their affinity group and you hold unto a job here while their member is jobless. The absurdity is part of their concern about you and why you are not good enough to keep a job with them. You must be a pauper not an interloper.

What is the complaint of you not wanting to be like them? You are not part of the team which is define as total, embarrassment, alleviation and a mouthful which makes it right to not participate. However, if the team is-trust, evaluate, access and maintain then you want to partake. The cause of complaint or concern of one choosing not to be like specific team (them) steps from the fact that a team which is seen as a total embarrassment, alleviation, involvement with unnecessary jokes or rumors of condescending facts gives you choice and right for nonparticipation. Notwithstanding if the team is trust-worthy, with evaluation, accesses interpersonal relationship as it pertain to the workplace and maintain cordial acceptable working atmosphere then you will want to participate. Everyone knows the perseverance of a workplace has a taciturn demeanor that challenges freedom and capability of people. There is no winner or loser.

What is the different about gratitude between people not of the same affinity group? No difference by heritage but by aversion in a tone of appreciation.

Therefore, gratitude is a bit to throw or to have norm in control of condition with the hope for decency. Saying thanks to a cashier at the end of line in a supermarket after checking your grocery for payment is gratitude. Our mental disposition enables us to refurbish our gratitude in every action of our recognizance of honesty.

Affinity group influence a lagging economic indicator when they are randomly selected based on a tacit instrument of offering jobs to silent them. This silence shows vested interest is not the same as altruistic interest in morality.

To live for accommodation in a certain locale is convenience for identity.

An echo by Walter Mosley in his book, (Devil in a Blue Dress,1990). Easy Rawlins a fiction character is unemployed and has a house with mortgage. He wants a job so his friend Joppy introduces him to a man who is willing to pay him if he can find Daphne. Here is how the man describes her. "You see, Easy, he cut me off, Daphne has a predilection for the company of Negroes. She likes jazz and pigs' feet and dark meat, if you know what I mean. I know but I didn't like to hear it. So you think she might be down around Watts." You know what you learn as a cause to sustain yourself does not wipe out of your memory even when you are penniless. Whenever you are in need of defense that thought comes back to remind you.

Why is settled assumption a cause for identity? Because people don't need many words to describe the relationship from the same race and having the same ancestry or speaking the same language. The action of people say it all as restriction to prevent others who do not have similar likeness and do not want to mix. But at a workplace people do mingled and it is not a mortal threat to their identity. The mixing is a routine to make sure that liberty is possible and not an estrangement. This impediment is always in a parallel direction.

Because every conceivable purpose is valuable and there is a standard to be applied. Such an indivisible wholeness is bewildered by experience from sensation of evidence that is profoundly personal.

Where is the burden of affinity groups? The acceptance of belonging and adjusting for your essential in a situation for empowerment. The resentment to be separate and equal. No group wants to be a guilty bystander of their non-sequitur behavior. For empowerment enables each group to be protective and defend their instinct. This self-assurance rests on what we want to seek out for ourselves and not be bother with others.

Why to be separate and equal is a challenge? It is a mandate usually taken when the time is ripe. A hold on you or the group to act and look beyond the presence of mind. You can observe that people move together through thick and thin with people they are comfortable with.

In 1954, the Supreme Court made a decision on Brown V. Board of Education.

This entrapment is a clue to what Juan Williams said in his book, (Enough, 2006). "The Brown decision itself is an example of black American leadership focused on self-determination, in this case the right to get an equal share of tax dollar to educate their children. A deliberate strategy of attacking segregation in graduate and professional schools led to the challenge against segregation in elementary and secondary schools and a victory in Brown." The credulousness of this burden is self-prescription that has been demanded and secured by the Commerce Clause in the constitution. We the people can not outstretched our hands in freedom and request help me from our foe. We must look to be invisible within the shadow of liberty.

Why is liberty the protective device for people at the workplace? For the consideration of the exceptional power to keep people in conformity and close proximity for any action in favor of morality. There should be no excuse in the suspension of liberty if malice may occurred at a workplace.

What is to care about in a workplace? The limitations and the spiteful excuses that are well defined and demanded as rules and regulations promulgated by companies. These procedures become drudgery when they produce silent and discomfort to the people about their performance. Most of the people will insist such proclamation is a way to doubt their loyalty. This surrealism is a glaring fact in the exchange of morality.

How to care without aversions in a workplace? Handling the consistency of denial when people do not want to engage themselves into the very thing that brings prosperity. People have to be ready to avoid any ineptitude used like the present condition of mixing people is not a reality. No change will come if work and relationship are not a mutual commitment from the company and the workers.

A desire to act, behave and sustain the importance of wanting to work is the foundation of talent. People must be willing to work for a company and be happy to do it. When you don't have the talent to work for a company and you are there, it is a drain to the company. Now I saying talent is a capacity to have a know-how. The desire to make that available is on you. This desire is what you have and the mean for what you want.

Therefore, working under rage to understand what is expected of us, is the premise of this book. It is a conditional factor at any workplace for coping..

WHOOP

To FORETELL WHAT WILL HAPPEN and it happens is a credit to necessity. But to do this is a courage an individual has to take when you know it is right. Hoping when that change comes for replacing the old for the new is not a problem. I want to whoop it up against degradation because some people believe it is a moral condition for others but not them. This outcry is valid whenever certain people are ashamed of their success and failure at the expense of others.

Should a workplace be just to have an income and benefits? Yes! The decision is not an end in itself but a succor for the existence of workers and companies.

This succor can be effluence at both level if creativity is a trait that must be encourage. I know some individual will not agree with me because they want the workplace to be their home. An illusion that hurts and may lead to mental issues when you retire from the workplace.

How refinement in work fits in the economic engine of Lincoln Industries? The choice is in the strategic objectives of the Beliefs and Drivers. These living propositions are use for encouraging the workers to engage in providing quality products to customers on time with added value service. Maintaining the core competency to become competitive in the market place. Securing cost to manage income, revenue and profit making. As a result, every refinement must be reliable for the strategic objectives to be awesome. If not, there will be change in the allocation for provisions in the budget during the fiscal year.

A point of resuscitation from a book by Jim Collins, (Good to Great, 2001).

"The Hedgehog Concept requires a severe standard of excellence. It's not just about building on strength and competence, but about understanding what your organization truly has the potential to be very best at and sticking to it." This ultimatum has been part of the historicity of Lincoln Industries proving that change is part of doing business. A factor that haunts the company daily to remain competitive.

Can the genetic makeup of specific affinity group in a company be consistent in behavior and thinking? Yes, the construct made by people must come from their affinity group to determine who they are. Some individual have a belief that the genetic make-up should not be mix at the workplace. A very important argument for being separate and equal.

My doubt about such belief is interaction leads to relationship which alter the behavior and thinking of people at a workplace. It is a known fact that inter- racially exists in the workplace. Who we are not who we want to be, is a retention of certain affinity groups in a workplace. Any act of no dilution preserves delusion echo inheritance by fixation; this meaning something that is factual needs to be separate and equal in genetics. The behavior and thinking of some people will be well as long as they are not depending on others for their survival.

We know this is self-evident when change is not merely a virtue but only a way of trying to get our preference which should be not difficult. The way to measure how people use their behavior and thinking at the workplace to manage resources-can be in-their conviction. This undertaking is a concern for some people in a company to oppose that the existing of a genetics drift will be an extinction of their affinity group if they do mix. With such belief is not to have an intersection where the chance to meet will be only a cry to preserve their identity. Preference is a conditional factor as the way to address these culprits.

Can behavior and thinking profiles of the people of Lincoln Industries be measured? Yes. According to what I am saying in this book emerge from the genetic and preferred pattern that I inspect for what I expect. The bottom line is people will do what is suitable and reliable as a challenge to overcome their discernible trait. Having all people of various affinity groups represented is important in every business setting to build a wholesome functioning company.

Now, there is a wall with pictures of many people who have been working at Lincoln Industries from 25 years to 46 years. The purpose of this picturesque wall shows gratitude to them for their commitment and possession of the value that enabled them in making a choice to have a relationship with this company.

This is also an indication that their working experience signifies their passion for being part of the company. The wall is a place for such recognition of gender and affinity groups and shows the mixture of people with such conduct that leaves the imprint of too many experiences of happy memories.

The faces of those people are more readily the comity of all affinity groups with values than command of repulsion. New people want to be acquainted with them to learn the challenge of how to work and retain an admration for the company. An empathy of admiration for the company in search of liberty in employment at will. For so many years those individuals had to work under rage to understand what was expected of them and still have fun within the workplace.

Let us take a look at some of the problems caused by diversity and inter- dependence of people at a workplace. To challenge people to recognize there is a difference in behaving and thinking in a workplace of people from different background. The result is the adaptation yet not letting go what has made them who they are not what they want to be.

It is a definite fact that do people want to protect the affinity group in regard to genetic drift? Yes. In the book by

John P. Kotter, (Power And Influence,1985). "Our cultural (religious and moral) roots and our biological roots go back many thousand years. These forces make people feel uncomfortable in modern organizations. These forces lead us to dream about dropping out, finding a simple life, moving to a cabin in the mountain or onto a small farm." The fear of losing our heritage whether we are majority or minority in a workplace comes from disillusionment and anxiety that there is no freedom in liberty. We must stop viewing our affinity group as the only group where belonging is to manage the values of our tenets. We are to use our desire to grow up and treat each other better for human decency.

Temptation is the rule of ethics that holds us back from making the choice to choose. This is how the interloper feels when the line is drawn that you can do all you can and play by the rules but you will not receive the reward of loyalty. You must nobly hide your agony and move on to challenge yourself to make your choice for destiny. You are alone in a relationship which is naught but a promise. This makes you know that self-reliance is a most worthy virtue of all the other virtues at that undetermined moment.

When is the moment of reckoning is realized? To unmask the illusion of what is holding you back from achieving your share of want. Do not keep on waiting to go beneath the surface before you exhale. Embracing the challenge is the only way forward. An exemplification echoed by Ralph Ellison in his book, (Invisible Man, 1952).

A student at Tuskegee University could not lie to a trustee about the deplorable living of some black people in a cabin next to the school. And the student should not have taken the trustee to the Golden Day-a sinkhole, a whorehouse, a bar and where he was treated by a Veteran for his illness. The president of the University was not happy and said this to the student. "My God, boy! You're black and living in the South-did you forget how to lie? But I was only trying to please him. Please him. And here you are a junior in college! Why the dumbest black bastard in the cotton patch knows that the only way to please a white man is to tell him a lie!."

Why must people lie? Ashamed of themselves or whatever they are doing is a masquerade. Lying becomes a problem of morality and is connected with those who are perplexed by the consequence of their own doubt. Again, I want to use the story of the student from Tuskegee University and its President. "I want you to go to New York for the summer and save your pride-and your money… I'll give you letters to some of the school's friend to see that you get work, he said. But this time, use your judgment, keep your eyes open, get in the swing of things! Then, if you make good, perhaps, It's up to you."

After his arrival in New York the student distributed six letters with no response. He changed his method of just giving the letter to wanting to see the philanthropist. This approach revealed the lies when the seventh letter was given to the son of the philanthropist who read the letter and returned it for the student to read for himself.

After reading the letter he was aware of why the other philanthropists never replied. He was expelled because he had exposed the hidden misery.

As I try to say in this book, we have to work under rage to understand what is expected as a desire of choice. Every day people want to decide what they believe is best for someone else but not themselves. The outcry at any place is let liberty be the guide. I know many people of the affinity group which I am part of do not like to look beneath the surface of racism as a curse within our heritage. We who are descendants must be willing to challenge ourselves and face the reality of our biases. We know it to be self-evidence that our doubt has a hold on us when degradation comes from our own kin.

Sometimes many writers make the point so clear that you can see it but refused to accept it.

This book should be a journey that I choose and there are no regret for spending those years with Lincoln Industries. If there is anything which may be painful is the misuse of opportunity by some people who may be angry for what I see as a taxpayer not an indentured servant but a Nebraskan with virtue.

Everything must come to the end, I am a senior citizen with a new beginning. At Lincoln Industries, the settled assumption may change if people make a conscious reliable and choices somewhere along the way. I must whoop it up for all those who go to work every day to improve the road of those propositions called the Beliefs and Drivers.

How long should the undetermined moment be available for a choice? The careful timing of freedom. I have come to the end of this book which was about my reexamination of work and affinity groups relation at Lincoln Industries. Thank you for taking your time to read it. I want to write again but on a different topic.

I want to repeat what my mother (Kieh Tih Taplah) said in the Kru language-Sa chlede jepo et et mu succlubo bip chlede jepo co wa mun bo. Translation, I don't know about (book) education. Therefore, you go to school and learn for all of us.

ACKNOWLEDGMENT

EVERY THOUGHT IN THIS BOOK rests on my shoulder and I am responsible for it entirety including the appearance. I thank my sister and editor Cecelia W. Kieh Nemah for the proofreading of the correlation coefficient of workmanship and affinity groups at Lincoln Industries upon my revelation. The trope of whatever I had said, is my indebtedness to my sixteen years and counting of being a hourly labor at that company. I am still working while this book is published.

Thanks to the folowing people for exemplifying the kind of work they do and to tolerate me for asking many questions. Andy Hunzeker, Bill Ellerbee, Bruce Brady, Casey Pflanz, Clint Boothe, Frank Cooper, Dennis Cash, Dennis Buckbee, Howard Tegtmeir, Jeff Holm, Joyce Person, Katie Haszard, Loi Vo, Marc LeBaron, Melaine Nebesniak, Norma Hardle, Steve Bauer, Tom Pryor, and Trevor Hanson.

Thanks to Hank Orme for listening to me with enthusiasm about my thought of Lincoln Industries and Laurence James for employment.

Thanks to those individuals for their comments about their dislikes which I accept as advice and consent.

Thanks and remembrance of two deceased friends, Chad Callahan and Michael LeBaron who had worked tirelessly for Lincoln Industries with pride, dignity and dedication.

BIBLIOGRAPHY

Bell, Derrick. Faces At The Bottom Of The Well: The Permanence of Racism, New York, Basic Books, 1992

Cook, Philip J. and Robert H. Frank. The Winner-Take-All Society: Why the Few at the Top Get So Much More Than the Rest of Us. New York, Penguin Books, 1995

Collins, Jim. Good To Great: Why Some Companies Make the Leap... and Others Don't. New York, Harper Collins Publishers, 2001.

Cose, Ellis. The Rage of A Privileged Class. New York, Harper Collins Publishers, 1993

Ehrenreich, Barbara. Nickel and Dimed: On (not) Getting by in America. New York, Henry Holt and Company, 2001.

Ellison, Ralph. Invisible Man. New York, Random House Inc. 1952

Hooks, Bell. Killing Rage: Ending Racism. New York, Henry Holt and Company, 1995.

Kant, Immanuel. Lectures On Ethics. London, Methuen and company, 1930.

Kotter, John P. Power and Influence. New York, The Free Press, 1985.

Morrison, Toni. Home. New York, Vintage Books, 2012

Mosley, Walter. Devil In A Blue Dress. New York, Washington Square Press, 1990

Murray, Albert. The Omni-Americans. New York, Random House Inc., 1970

Shelby, Tommie. We Who Are Dark: The Philosophical Foundation of Black Solidarity. Masssachusetts, Harvard University Press, 2005

Theriault, Reg. How to Tell When You're Tired: A Brief Examination of Work. New York, W.W. Norton and Company, 1995.

West, Cornel. Race Matters, Boston, Beacon Press, 1993.

Williams, Juan. Enough: The Phony Leaders, Dead-End Movements, and Culture of Failure That Are Undermining Black America-and What We Can Do about It. New York, Crown Publishers, 2006.